ESSENCE

NOEL ANDREWS

To lovers

Contents

Contents

1. ANGELS OF THE HEART

The angels sent a message,
The good Lord insisted,
And I cut through the prime of my life,
With a sharp blade of loneliness and sacrifice,
Until the time was ripe and life slipped out of,
A common hand too old to grasp,
The young and lively strands of life again,
And I wept unnoticed in my igloo,
For months and years with soft hands,
Caressing my back,
Yet my home far away in snow,
Is aglow with hearts that long for me.

2. ANONYMOUSLY YOURS

A new world has been born,
The children are much like their forefathers,
There is a sudden rush of people at the train stations,
In malls, colleges, parks and on the streets,
They have inherited the same frame of mind,
Much like the people of the past,
Albeit there is greater fear to waver from the path,
The children hate the timeless philosophy,
Of a bracketed life with a stipulated future,
Yet no one has the courage to break the bracket,
It's not that people earlier did anything different,
But this time there is a stronger tether to the norm.

3. BURNING MODEL

I was burning in a thick fire,

My being melting into something new,

It was getting unbearable and never ending,

While the world slipped into swanky cafes,

And those marble cakes and fragrant cappuccinos,

You cannot feel the dead man that just walked by,

He's slipped into clothes that reveal a bulging inner,

Don't pause your carnival with an ungainly sight,

That man has dreams too,

Has anyone heard the sound of wet clay,

The Artist is hard at work while the model stands still,

The coffee crowd do marvel at the finished work.

4. CHAINS

The young ones love chains,
They's rather be entangled in them forever,
It's like a vicious cycle with no different fate,
Like their forefathers and their forefathers,
Where then is the room for something different,
Who has the courage to break the monotony of cycles,
Perhaps a cruel earth could swallow you if you did,
Don't try to fight the beast in you,
It could tear your life into smithereens,
And leave you into the forests of loneliness,
To such an extent that your cries are your own,
They provide you great comfort and fun in your cells.

5. CONSTANT MOULD

I bent low on heavy knees joining hands,

In a silent prayer for my plight so,

My eyes of water pushed by a wink,

Into the hollows of cold cheeks,

Some people like the pole star,

Hurt and sadden in a lingering pain,

Some that God transfixed in the pattern of my life,

And cannot be shrugged or sorted,

Washed by an ocean of wisdom,

They forget the word by night,

The spark out of flint of friction I see,

It's moulding me still.

6. DAMP SQUIB

Don't run the risk of sharing your joy,
With people who cannot be with you,
In your world of dreams and triumphs,
Fatherless sons these are poised on new wines,
A new life each day to erase stains of slavery,
That they succumbed to suffer the cost of freedom,
Tacky gaits borrowed from men of steel,
Trying to hide an impudent mind,
That shall pinch with a weather of doom,
The lanky dude and wobbling eyes of pricey dames,
Until the soft tethers of slavery,
That is taking them deep into the alleged abyss.

7. DIFFERENT STROKES

There are people that move the earth,
There are those that fear the deep,
There are still those that have not moved,
And surrendered to the nook of safety,
There are those that embellish and adorn,
Their looks and a darkening physical,
There are those that expel their guts,
And let out the poison in their hearts,
There are some that shall never speak,
And let the poison spread throughout,
Carrying an ocean of negativity,
Until the great capsize.

8. FATHER'S WORDS

My father never told me,
What victory meant,
How far one must go to reach the very end,
My faults and inabilities spoke louder than me,
They followed me until the sweet incense,
When the Almighty spoke of my struggles,
And how I had fared in the fair,
My father turned out to be my saviour,
When he said that I was never quite there,
Like the work shall never be done,
And so, I pushed myself higher than dizzy,
To end in a world that had hardly been touched.

9. FREE FLOWING

I have stepped into timelessness,
I am stuck in a haloed place called heaven,
I feel each day as new,
Like a span of excitement of learning,
That busy street is miles away I see,
Even with a deafening noise right at my nose,
The Voice reveals facts that are astounding,
It is discussing the plight of the human civilization,
My love likes to have coffee by sunset,
She smiles at me and urges me to carry on,
My words are like an endless stream of river water,
They are my Holy Bible lending a torch light to my despair.

10. GREATEST PHILANTHROPIST

The rich ones are blessed,

With pockets of glistening gold,

In their season of glory,

A new one turns into a great philanthropist,

Not aware where exactly that stream seeped through,

Not knowing the names of the people thus benefitted,

The greatest charity is that of the human soul,

When it shines in the eyes of the giver,

And breaks the long drought of sadness and misery,

Albeit for a moment or two,

When the hands of the giver are one with the taker,

Surprising then the poorest are the greatest philanthropist.

11. HOLY MOTHER

Storms of dust leaves a land of spittoon,
A constant nag leaves imprints on travellers,
Or those hobo gypsies that detest water,
A swish of hands when eyes begin to water,
Clean clothes are a dream for many,
For this is the Holy land,
The gush of dust are Mother's hands,
She wants to feel the feather on her cap,
As many have left Her in a hurtful Diaspora,
And many leave her ignoring Her cries,
I stand stiff when the dust ball paints my face,
I cannot ever give back Her gift of a heart.

12. HUSH WORLDS

I saw a hobo and followed him,
I saw great stairs and columns of Rome,
I saw a young girl in red,
Like the one I had seen before,
I saw a woman after fifty years,
I sat in a room with curtains of hushed tapestry,
I have heard of waters clear as glass,
With discoloured rocks and dank fishes,
Visible to the eye,
Sometimes I wonder what the world is after,
For I am convinced of a world beyond this world,
For my father spoke with his eyes for most.

13. I AM AMAZED

My eyes in tears,

To see my mother old and struggling,

I promised myself to never leave her alone,

My sorrow too deep to even think of myself,

I walked miles in the dead of the night,

My feet dragged me like a kiss of death,

To find the missing pill in her armoury of medicines,

I was the morning tea man,

She loved to start her day with tea,

We travelled far and wide around the city,

She liked new dresses and look prim,

She became a child with passing age,

Ready and obliging at the smallest of requests,

She poured out her heart in the form of stories,

She often was in tears talking about her parents,

I loved her and she quietly gave up her life for me,

God snatched away everything from me,

After she was gone too soon,

She was the last one I knew in this world,

I live alone now, lost and abandoned,

I have no dreams or a family,

I am a man with no means or wealth,

The poorest one perhaps in the world,

I just have one question for every man and woman,

Given the turmoil that we live in today,
Has anyone experienced love ever in their life,
Has anyone loved anyone ever in their lives,
Being grown up doesn't necessarily mean,
Being brutish and wild in passionate lust,
Scoring high in an illicit love,
Love is a simple thing,
It is not a monster that we must tame,
And love is not meant for everyone, sadly,
For it is a fire that each one must avoid.

14. LAST MERCY

I asked the Lord why this hatred,
Why should a man love and not hate,
I have seen huge rocks and boulders,
Like on the pages of a book by the river,
Lifeless remnants of a stolen kingdom,
I have shared the huddles of warmth and love,
Of my parents and a light banter,
Wisdom is the bailer when you lose someone,
For I have made the fatal error of facing the wind,
My boat is weathered and beaten,
I am on the last mercy of God,
The rocks shall never speak.

15. LOVELY GUESTS

Sun rays of orange and purple,
Mingle in the air on a sunny morning,
And some delightful guests hop on the cold porch,
They pick and prick a pinch of soil,
I sit like a statue on my veranda,
To create an air of silence and stillness,
The flowers yellow and red are in complete bloom,
They bunch together like on a maiden's tress,
The squirrels have found a safe zone on the porch,
They diddle and dabble to sharpen their teeth,
I hear the birds chirp and twitter something sweet,
How can I thank God for making me the last in the chain.

16. MISSING STRETCH

The caravan of melody receding in the distance,
Is not a simple jingle,
To casually set aside,
Billow of negative dust churn in the stomach,
Each time the remnants of the caravan,
Fall into ears of swish,
And then a sudden darkness before the eyes,
To dissolve the moment that spun,
And will spin again a thousand times,
And to think that we are a breath away,
From apples of red and season of green,
Is to erase the scorching battlefield called life.

17. MY REGRETS

My biggest regret are the words I just said,
Thoughts cloud my mind of what could have been,
These are my sins that shall hurt,
Like deeds in a life of beams and balances,
What I said I did may not be true,
For who is to gauge my actions,
I am doomed with no hands to reconcile me,
For this is a world of records and accounts,
Of things done and not done,
Kept by keen Hands,
There are those that are masters of manoeuvring,
They could fool the Higher if they could.

18. NO ANGELS IN SIGHT

I found no angels of kindness,
Like the remnants of a past life,
That sought to haunt and ruin my present,
There can be other reasons than love,
When women like witches seek to pitch a tent,
In the inner of my heart,
And mingle with the warmth of my body,
Speaking in a language that they call sublime,
Or that I hail from a near affluent family,
Making an exception as my pocket with a hole,
I was almost drowned with only my hands above the waters,
But I did not perish at the hands of garbage women.

19. NO QUESTIONS PLEASE

I am perched among the clouds,
I see young ones don heavy coats,
Perplexed with questions in motion,
The constant chatter,
Occasionally someone releases the tight air,
This façade of fake confidence,
Will capture the slippery footsteps to a corner,
Like someone knows the answers until the oil runs out,
Take adults that toyed with the questionnaire,
Dodging and dismissing the semblance of a test,
Sitting in a dark cocoon that's has enough supplies,
Of colourful fruits of the season.

20. THE DARK AGE

The stone age did hurt us for long,
Until someone conjured up the magic wheel,
Human challenging the breeze with little effort,
God blessed his children with a brain,
And humans erected a world out of logic,
Until it created huge gaps to overpower the other,
The physical body took a beating with reduced mobility,
Giving rise to fatal diseases from lack of harness,
Technology was a new word humans invented,
It created a sick generation of passive users,
Jealousy, greed, treachery, wastage became common,
Values so low pushed God to create hell.

21. THE DOME

I changed the dome in foots of swift,
I faced the devil with a drop of insane,
But I did not end my life as some do,
God's challenges like a sticky swarm of bees,
To rip the stitches of the skin in anger,
A million times I did cry to be rushed to mad houses,
And God urged my soul to forgive, which I did,
They are still brewing gaps in my speech for provocation,
To rush me to the aisles of rescue mills,
Those dark people have already been siphoned to hell,
I sit with an army of silence,
To walk too far into the closet of my footsteps.

22. THE GARDEN

I walked past the jungle to arrive at this garden,
It is the garden of my dreams,
A soft rush of breeze,
And the flowers and leaves utter in silence,
In snippets before standing still again,
This is indeed the final chapter,
Of my journey through uneven ground and pods of ivy,
The world has woken up to a new morning,
They have made plans for the day,
They have a thirst that cannot be quenched,
Not even in a hundred,
Hence the Almighty let them have it.

23. THE MESSAGE

Leave me a whiff of your glory,
Walk through a seamless path endlessly,
Bear the thorns in your passage,
Without stains of blood in a soft brush,
Walk calmy through the blemished crossroads,
Without wearing a cloak of ages,
Of a killer that must plunder and kill,
Be brave enough to capture a solemn mountain,
In your hurried footsteps of impatience,
Don't spill the life in your soul too soon,
Don't utter a word until the very end,
Untie and rip, the moon wishes to sink for good.

24. THE MYSTERY

When life is more than a pre-arranged plan,
Like a motley family at the breakfast table,
When you slip out of parties like strangers without a noise,
When the wind, trees, roads and skies don't seem to know you,
When time is perhaps is the only one aware,
Of subtle shifts in a useless piece of earth,
When the buzz of the present of a busy day,
Shows no sign of anything worthwhile happening,
When you are far away from life,
For reasons not your own making,
Like the lack of masculinity,
Then you have come close to unlocking the mystery of life.

25. TRANSFORMATION

Ten years of picketed roam,
On burnt soil and trees not worthy of,
My thoughts singular on merchants of beauty,
A hot bed of dos and don'ts matching reality,
Yet something was alive in me through all those years,
Deepest actions yet unknown to my mind,
Yet it somehow formed a remarkable pattern,
I was being led even with temptations too strong,
From ladies that crushed the fragments of a broken heart,
My mind and body like fickle bubbles,
In a pot of hot boiling water,
And the pot never gave up for ages.

26. TRUTH HARDLY MATTERS

Love is a hidden truth,

Hate is alive in the blowing wind,

We live behind thick curtains,

Of numbness and the dry desert,

In emptiness of scars and torments,

Of things that shall not reveal itself,

Of people that lie dead in our hearts,

God speaks to us in the language of signs,

He lets time expel the truth in the final chapter,

A truth that should have been known much earlier,

We are a generation of sleeping people,

Our forty winks are dearer than the truth.

27. WHAT HAPPENED TO

Why do the flowers look pale,
What happened to the warmth of the skies,
On a day of clear blue,
Why is the bright not so bright anymore,
When the sun sails in oceans of blue,
What happened to the melodies we used to hear,
Silly and sweet with words of rhyme,
That didn't make sense and don't do still,
Why don't words echo flutter of hearts,
Like emptying a fresh pale of water,
Instead of being drowned in gasps of fear,
Funny that some things will never change.

28. WHERE IS THE WALTZ

See the old folks waltzing,
Their hearts are than of young,
While the young ones have no clue,
Their feet have no rhythm for dancing,
They are walking an unknown terrain,
Too old already in a sick mind and body,
The sound of music and the beads of a poem,
Have no meaning as they get too close to love,
When the heat off their bodies begin to stink,
The old ones have begun to sweat,
They can sense the hot stuff in the swinging melody,
'Come join in, you fools, in life you got to twist and shout.

29. WHERE'S HELL

Suddenly the gates were opened,

And in rushed a mammoth crowd,

Every inch of earth set to suffer bondage,

There are more people with empty bowls,

Too hungry for food amidst the growing squalor,

Death and disease scribbled on walls and the pockets of air,

Each one perishing to an unheard ailment,

Doctors are an encyclopaedia of deadly disease,

They are warning each one for their actions,

The rich ones fool themselves to be totally safe,

Their inners are ripping apart the sick organs,

As they consume unheard drugs for some more breath.

30. WHERE'S THE WEDDING

My wedding day was imminent,
I waited for it ever since I turned seventeen,
Many girls on their stoops passed my gaze,
In all readiness to enter my world,
My parents dodged the matter for too long,
As if marriage were a sin,
I stuck to being holy for years on end,
To the extent of an emerging priesthood in me,
My father left me with pretensions of a suitable bride,
Waiting for me back home while I was away,
My mother finally gave in to popular demand,
And I was betrothed that lasted for thirty days,
Without performing the sacred act,
They accused of a crime I had not committed,
Until I slipped into my fifties,
My mother left me without a wish,
And I was never married until the end.